Sutherland As It Was And Is...

Hugh Miller

1820, fifteen thousand inhabitants of this northern district were ejected from their snug inland farms, by means for which we would in vain seek a precedent, except, perchance, in the history of the Irish massacre. But though the interior of the county was thus *improved* into a desert, in which there are many thousands of sheep, but few human habitations, let it not be supposed by the reader that its general population was in any degree lessened. So far was this from being the case, that the census of 1821 showed an increase over the census of 1811 of more than two hundred; and the present population of Sutherland exceeds, by a thousand, its population before the change. The county has not been depopulated,—its population has been merely arranged after a new fashion. The late Duchess found it spread equally over the interior and the sea-coast, and in very comfortable circumstances;—she left it compressed into a wretched selvage of poverty and suffering, that fringes the county on its eastern and western shores. And the law which enabled her to make such an arrangement, maugre the ancient rights of the poor Highlander, is now on the eve of stepping in, in its own clumsy way, to make her family pay the penalty. The evil of a poor-law can be no longer averted from Scotland. However much we may dislike compulsory assessment for the support of our poor, it can be no longer avoided. Our aristocracy have been working hard for it during the whole of the present century, and a little longer; the disruption of the Scottish Church, as the last in a series of events, all of which have tended towards it, has rendered it inevitable. Let the evidence of the present Commissioners on the subject be what it may, it cannot be of a kind suited to show that if England should have a poor-law, Scotland should have none. The southern kingdom must and will give us a poor-law; and then shall the selvage of deep poverty which fringes the sea-coasts of Sutherland avenge on the titled proprietor of the county both his mother's error and his own. If our British laws, unlike those of Switzerland, failed miserably in *her* day in protecting the vassal, they will more than fail in those of her successor, in protecting the lord. Our political economists shall have an opportunity of reducing their arguments regarding the improvements in Sutherland into a few arithmetical terms, which the merest tyro will be able to grapple with.

We find a similar case thus strongly stated by Cobbett in his Northern Tour, and in connection with a well-known name:—" Sir James Graham has his estate lying off this road to the left. He has not been *clearing* his estate,—the poor-law would not let him do that; but he has been clearing off the small farms, and making them into large ones, which he had a right to do, because it is he himself that is finally to endure the consequences of that: he has a right to do that; and those who are made indigent in consequence of his so doing, have a right to demand a maintenance out of the land, according to act of the 43d of Elizabeth, which gave the people a COMPENSATION for the loss of the tithes and Church lands which had been taken away by the aristocracy in the reigns of the Tudors. If Sir James Graham choose to mould his fine and large estate into immense farms, and to break up numerous happy families in the middle rank of life, and to expose them all to the necessity of coming and demanding sustenance from his estate; if he choose to be surrounded by masses of persons in this state, he shall not call them *paupers*, for that insolent term is not to be found in the compensation-laws of Elizabeth; if he choose to be surrounded by swarms of be-ings of this description, with feelings in their bosoms towards him such as I need not describe,—if he choose this, his RIGHT certainly extends thus far; but I tell him that he has no right to say to any man born in his parishes,—' You shall not be here, and you shall not have a main-tenance off these lands.' "

There is but poor comfort, however, to know, when one sees a coun-try ruined, that the perpetrators of the mischief have not ruined it to their own advantage. We purpose showing how signal in the case of Sutherland this ruin has been, and how very extreme the infatuation which continues to possess its hereditary lord. We are old enough to re-member the county in its original state, when it was at once the happiest and one of the most exemplary districts in Scotland, and passed, at two several periods, a considerable time among its hills; we are not unac-quainted with it now, nor with its melancholy and dejected people, that wear out life in their comfortless cottages on the sea-shore. The pro-blem solved in this remote district of the kingdom is not at all unworthy the attention which it seems but beginning to draw, but which is al-ready not restricted to one kingdom, or even one continent.

CHAPTER II.

WE heard sermon in the open air with a poor Highland congrega-tion in Sutherlandshire only a few weeks ago; and the scene was one which we shall not soon forget. The place of meeting was a green hill side, near the opening of a deep, long withdrawing strath, with a river running through the midst. We stood on the slope where the last of a line of bold eminences that form the southern side of the valley, sinks towards the sea. A tall precipitous mountain, reverend and hoary, and well fitted to tranquillize the mind, from the sober solemnity that rests on its massy features, rose fronting us on the north; a quiet burial-ground lay at its feet; while, on the opposite side, between us and the sea, there frowned an ancient stronghold of time-eaten stone,—an im-pressive memorial of an age of violence and bloodshed. The last pro-prietor, says tradition, had to quit this dwelling by night, with all his family, in consequence of some unfortunate broil, and take refuge in a small coasting vessel; a terrible storm arose,—the vessel foundered at sea,—and the hapless proprietor and his children were never more heard of. And hence, it is said, the extinction of the race.

The story speaks of an unsettled time; nor is it difficult to trace, in the long deep valley on the opposite hand, the memorials of a story not less sad, though much more modern. On both sides the river the eye rests on a multitude of scattered patches of green, that seem inlaid in the brown heath. We trace on these islands of sward, the marks of furrows, and mark here and there, through the loneliness, the remains of a group of cottages, well nigh levelled with the soil, and, haply like those ruins which eastern conquerors leave in their track, still scathed with fire. All is solitude within the valley, except where, at wide intervals, the shieling of a shepherd may be seen ; but at its opening, where the hills range to the coast, the cottages for miles together lie clustered as in a hamlet. From the north of Helmsdale to the south of Port Gower, the lower slopes of the hills are covered by a labyrinth of stone fences, minute patches of corn, and endless cottages. It would seem as if for twenty miles the long withdrawing valley had been swept of its inhabitants, and the accumulated sweepings left at its mouth, just as we see the sweepings of a room sometimes left at the door. And such generally is the present state of Sutherland. The interior is a solitude occupied by a few sheep-farmers and their hinds ; while a more numerous population than fell to the share of the entire county, ere the inhabitants were expelled from their inland holdings, and left to squat upon the coast, occupy the selvage of discontent and poverty that fringes its shores. The congregation with which we worshipped on this occasion was drawn mainly from these cottages, and the neighbouring village of Helmsdale. It consisted of from six to eight hundred Highlanders, all devoted adherents of the Free Church. We have rarely seen a more deeply serious assemblage ; never certainly one that bore an air of such deep dejection. The people were wonderfully clean and decent,—for it is ill with Highlanders when they neglect their personal appearance, especially on a Sabbath ; but it was all too evident that the heavy hand of poverty rested upon them, and that its evils were now deepened by oppression. It might be a mere trick of association ; but when their plaintive Gaelic singing, so melancholy in its tones at all times, arose from the bare hill-side, it sounded in our ears like a deep wail of complaint and sorrow. Poor people ! " We were ruined and reduced to beggary before," they say, " and now the gospel is taken from us."

Nine-tenths of the poor people of Sutherland are adherents of the Free Church,—all of them in whose families the worship of God has been set up,—all who entertain a serious belief in the reality of religion, —all who are not the creatures of the proprietor, and have not stifled their convictions for a piece of bread,—are devotedly attached to the disestablished ministers, and will endure none other. The Residuary clergy they do not recognise as clergy at all. The Established churches have become as useless in the district, as if, like its Druidical circles, they represented some idolatrous belief, long exploded,—the people will not enter them ; and they respectfully petition his Grace to be permitted to build other churches for themselves. And fain would his Grace indulge them, he says. In accordance with the suggestions of an innate desire, willingly would he permit them to build their own churches and support their own ministers. But then, has he not loyally engaged to support the Establishment ? To permit a religious and inoffensive people to build their own places of worship, and support their own clergy, would be sanctioning a sort of persecution against the Establishment ; and as his Grace dislikes religious persecution, and has determined always to oppose whatever tends to it, he has resolved to make use of his influence, as the most extensive of Scottish proprietors, in forcing them back to their parish churches. If they persist in worshipping God agreeably to the dictates of their conscience, it must be on the unsheltered hill-side,—in winter, amid the frosts and snows of a severe northern climate,—in the milder seasons, exposed to the scorching sun and the drenching shower. They must not be permitted the shelter of a roof, for that would be persecuting the Establishment; and so to the Establishment must the people be forced back, literally by stress of weather. His Grace owes a debt to the National Institution, and it seems to irk his conscience until some equivalent be made. He is not himself a member,—he exercises the same sort of liberty which his people would so fain exercise; and to make amends for daring to belong to another Church himself (that of England), he has determined, if he can help it, that the people shall belong to no other. He has resolved, it would seem, to compound for his own liberty by depriving them of theirs.

How they are to stand out the winter on this exposed eastern coast, He alone knows who never shuts his ear to the cry of the oppressed. One thing is certain,—they will never return to the Establishment. On this Sabbath the congregation in the parish church did not, as we afterwards learned, exceed a score; and the *quoad sacra* chapel of the district was locked up. Long before the disruption the people had well-nigh ceased attending the ministrations of the parish incumbent. The Sutherland Highlanders are still a devout people ;—they like a bald mediocre essay none the better for its being called a sermon, and read on Sabbath. The Noble Duke, their landlord, has said not a little in his letters to them about the extreme slightness of the difference which obtains between the Free and the Established Churches: it is a difference so exceedingly slight, that his Grace fails to see it ; and he hopes that by and by, when winter shall have thickened the atmosphere with its frost rhime and its snows, his poor tenantry may prove as unable to see it as himself. With them, however, the difference is not mainly a doctrinal one. They believe, with the old Earls of Sutherland, who did much to foster the belief in this northern county, that there is such a thing as personal piety,—that of two clergymen holding nominally the same doctrines, and bound ostensibly by the same standards, one may be a regenerate man, earnestly bent on the conversion of others, and ready to lay down his worldly possessions, and even life itself, for the cause of the gospel ; while the other may be an unregenerate man, so little desirous of the conversion of others, that he would but decry and detest them did he find them converted already, and so careless of the gospel, that did not his living depend on professing to preach it, he would neither be an advocate for it himself, nor yet come within earshot of where it was advocated by others. The Highlanders of Sutherland hold in deep seriousness a belief of this character. They believe, further, that the ministers of their own mountain district belong to these two classes,—that the disruption of the Scottish Church has thrown the classes apart,—that the Residuaries are not men of personal piety,—they have seen no conversions attending their ministry,—nor have they lacked reason to deem them unconverted themselves. Unlike his Grace the Duke, the people have been intelligent enough to see two sets of principles ranged in decided antagonism in the Church question ; but still more clearly have they seen two sets of men. They have identified the cause of the gospel with that of the Free Church in their district; and neither the Duke of Sutherland, nor the Establishment which he is " engaged in endeavouring to maintain," will be able to reverse the opinion."

We have said that his Grace's ancestors, the old Earls, did much to foster this spirit. The history of Sutherland, as a county, differs from all our other Highland districts. Its two great families were those of

Reay and Sutherland ; both of which, from an early period of the Reformation, were not only Protestant, but also thoroughly evangelical. It was the venerable Earl of Sutherland who first subscribed the National Covenant in the Greyfriars. It was a scion of the Reay family,—a man of great personal piety,—who led the troops of William against Dundee at Killiecrankie. Their influence was all-powerful in Sutherland, and directed to the best ends ; and we find it stated by Captain Henderson, in his general view of the agriculture of the country, as a well-established and surely not uninteresting fact, that " the crimes of rapine, murder, and plunder, though not unusual in the county during the feuds and conflicts of the clans, were put an end to about the year 1640,"—a full century before our other Highland districts had become even partially civilized. " Pious Earls and Barons of former times," says a native of the county, in a small work published in Edinburgh about sixteen years ago," encouraged and patronized pious ministers, and a high tone of religious feeling came thus to be diffused throughout the country." Its piety was strongly of the Presbyterian type ; and in no district of the south were the questions which received such prominence in our late ecclesiastical controversy, better understood by both the people and the patrons, than in Sutherland a full century ago. We have before us an interesting document, the invitation of the elders, parishioners, and heritors of Lairg, to the Rev. Thomas M'Kay, 1748, to be their minister, in which, " hoping that" he would find their " call, carried on with great sincerity, unanimity, and order, to be a clear call from the Lord," they faithfully promise to " yield him, in their several stations and relations, all dutiful respect and encouragement." William Earl of Sutherland was patron of the parish, but we find him on this occasion exercising no patronate powers : at the head of parishioners and elders he merely adhibits his name. He merely *invites* with the others. The state of morals in the county was remarkably exemplified at a later period by the regiment of Sutherland Highlanders, embodied originally in 1793, under the name of the Sutherlandshire Fencibles, and subsequently in 1800 as the 93d regiment. Most other troops are drawn from among the unsettled and reckless part of the population : not so the Sutherland Highlanders. On the breaking out of the revolutionary war, the mother of the present Duke summoned them from their hills, and five hundred fighting men marched down to Dunrobin Castle, to make a tender of their swords to their country, at the command of their chieftainess. The regiment, therefore, must be regarded as a fair specimen of the character of the district ; and from the description of General Stewart of Garth, and one or two sources besides, we may learn what that character was.

" In the words of a general officer, by whom they were once reviewed," says General Stewart, " they exhibited a perfect pattern of military discipline and moral rectitude." " When stationed at the Cape of Good Hope, anxious to enjoy the advantages of religious instruction agreeably to the tenets of their national Church, and there being no religious service in the garrison except the customary one of reading prayers to the soldiers on parade, the Sutherland men formed themselves into a congregation, appointed elders of their own number, engaged and paid a stipend (collected among themselves) to a clergyman of the Church of Scotland (who had gone out with an intention of teaching and preaching to the Caffres), and had Divine service performed agreeably to the ritual of the Established Church. * * In addition to these expenses, the soldiers regularly remitted money to their relatives in Sutherland. When they disembarked at Plymouth in August 1814, the inhabitants were both surprised and gratified. On such occasions it had been no uncommon thing for soldiers to spend in taverns and gin-shops the money they had saved. In the present case, the soldiers of Sutherland were seen in booksellers' shops, supplying themselves with Bibles, and such books and tracts as they required. Yet, as at the Cape, where their religious habits were so free of all fanatical gloom that they occasionally indulged in social meetings and dancing, so here, while expending their money on books, they did not neglect their personal appearance; and the haberdashers' shops had also their share of trade, from the purchase of additional feathers to their bonnets, and such extra decorations as the correctness of military regulations allow to be introduced into the uniform. Nor, while thus mindful of themselves,—improving their minds and their personal appearance,—did such of them as had relations in Sutherland forget their destitute condition, *occasioned by the loss of their lands,* and the operation of the *improved state of the country.* During the short period that the regiment was quartered at Plymouth, upwards of L.500 were lodged in one banking-house, to be remitted to Sutherland, exclusive of many sums sent through the Post Office and by officers. Some of the sums exceeded L.20 from an individual soldier."

" In the case of such men," continues the General, " disgraceful punishment was as unnecessary as it would have been pernicious. Indeed, so remote was the idea of such a measure in regard to them, that when punishments were to be inflicted on others, and the troops in camp, garrison, or quarters, assembled to witness their execution, the presence of the Sutherland Highlanders,—either of the fencibles or of the line,—was dispensed with; the effect of terror, as a check to crime, being in their case uncalled for, ' *as examples of that nature were not necessary for such honourable soldiers.*' Such were these men in garrison. How thoroughly they were guided by honour and loyalty in the field, was shown at New Orleans. Although many of their countrymen who had emigrated to America were ready and anxious to receive them, there was not an instance of desertion; nor did one of those who were left behind, wounded or prisoners, forget their allegiance and remain in that country,—at the same time that desertions from the British army were but too frequent."

This is testimony which even men of the world will scarce suspect. We can supplement it by that of the missionary whom the Sutherland-shire soldiers made choice of at Cape Town as their minister. We quote from a letter by the Rev. Mr Thom, which appeared in the *Christian Herald* of October 1814 :—

" When the 93d Sutherland Highlanders left Cape Town last month," writes the reverend gentleman, " there were among them 156 members of the Church (including three elders and three deacons), all of whom, so far as man can know the heart from the life, were pious persons. The regiment was certainly a pattern for morality and good behaviour to every other corps. They read their Bibles; they observed the Sabbath; they saved their money in order to do good; 7000 rix-dollars (L.1400 currency), the non-commissioned officers and privates gave for books, societies, and the support of the gospel,—a sum perhaps unparalleled in any other corps in the world, given in the short space of seventeen or eighteen months. Their example had a general good effect on both the colonists and the heathen. How they may act as to religion in other parts, is known to God; but if ever apostolic days were revived in modern times on earth, I certainly believe some of these to have been granted to us in Africa."

One other extract of a similar kind: we quote from a letter to the Committee of the Edinburgh Gaelic School Society,—Fourth Annual Report :—

" The regiment (93d) arrived in England, when they immediately received orders to proceed to North America; but before they re-embarked, the sum collected for your Society was made up, and has been remitted to your treasurer, amounting to seventy-eight pounds sterling."

We dwell with pleasure on this picture; and shall present the reader, in our next chapter, with a picture of similar character, taken from observation, of the homes in which these soldiers were reared. The reverse is all too stern, but we must exhibit *it* also, and show how the influence which the old Earls of Sutherland employed so well, has been exerted by their descendants to the ruin of their country. But we must first give one other extract from General Stewart. It indicates the tract in which the ruin came.

" Men like these," he says, referring to the Sutherland Highlanders, " do credit to the peasantry of the country. If this conclusion is well founded, the removal of so many of the people from their ancient seats, where they acquired those habits and principles, must be considered a public loss of no common magnitude. It must appear strange, and somewhat inconsistent, when the same persons who are loud in their professions of an eager desire to promote and preserve the religious and moral virtues of the people, should so frequently take the lead in approving of measures which, by removing them from where they imbibed principles which have attracted the notice of Europe, and placed them in situations where poverty, and the too frequent attendants, vice and crime, will lay the foundation for a character which will be a disgrace, as that already obtained has been an honour, to this country. In the new stations, where so many Highlanders are now placed, and crowded in such numbers as to preserve the numerical population, while whole districts are left without inhabitants, how can they resume their ancient character and principles, which, according to the reports of those employed by the proprietors, have been so deplorably broken down and deteriorated,—a deterioration which was entirely unknown till the recent change in the condition of the people, and the introduction of that system of placing families on patches of potato ground, as in Ireland,—a system pregnant with degradation, poverty, and disaffection, and exhibiting daily a prominent and deplorable example, which might have forewarned Highland proprietors, and prevented them from reducing their people to a similar state! It is only when parents and heads of families in the Highlands are moral, happy, and contented, that they can instil sound principles into their children, who, in their intercourse with the world, may once more become what the men of Sutherland have already been, ' an honourable example, worthy the imitation of all.' "

CHAPTER III.

WE have exhibited the Sutherland Highlanders to the reader as they exhibited themselves to their country, when, as Christian soldiers,—men, like the old chivalrous knight, " without fear or reproach,"—they fought its battles and reflected honour on its name. Interest must attach to the manner in which men of so high a moral tone were reared; and a sketch drawn from personal observation of the interior of Sutherland eight-and-twenty years ago, may be found to throw very direct light on the subject. To know what the district once was, and what it is now, is to know with peculiar emphasis the meaning of the sacred text,—" One sinner destroyeth much good."

The eye of a Triptolemus Yellowlee would have found exceedingly little to gratify it in the parish of Lairg thirty years ago. The parish had its bare hills, its wide, dark moors, its old doddered woods of birch and hazel, its extensive lake, its headlong river, and its roaring cataract. Nature had imparted to it much of a wild and savage beauty; but art had done nothing for it. To reverse the well-known antithesis in which Goldsmith sums up his description of Italy,—the only growth that had *not* dwindled in it was man. The cottage in which we resided with an aged relative and his two stalwart sons, might be regarded as an average specimen of the human dwellings of the district. It was a low, long building of turf, consisting of four apartments on the ground floor,—the one stuck on to the end of the other, and threaded together by a passage that connected the whole. From the nearest hill the cottage reminded one of a huge black snail crawling up the slope. The largest of the four apartments was occupied by the master's six milk cows; the next in size was the ha', or sitting room,—a rude but not uncomfortable apartment, with the fire on a large flat stone in the middle of the floor. The apartment, adjoining was decently partitioned into sleeping places; while the fourth and last in the range,—more neatly fitted up than any of the others, with furniture, the workmanship of a bred carpenter, a small book-case containing from forty to fifty volumes, and a box-bed of deal,—was known as the strangers' room. There was a straggling group of buildings outside, in the same humble style,—a stable, a barn, a hay-barn, a sheep-pen with a shed attached, and a milk-house; and stretching around the whole lay the farm,—a straggling patch of corn-land of from twelve to fifteen acres in extent, that, from its extremely irregular outline, and the eccentric forms of the party-coloured divisions into which it was parcelled, reminded one of a coloured map. Encircling all was a wide sea of heath studded with huge stones,—the pasturage land of the farmer for his sheep and cattle,—which swept away on every hand to other islands of corn and other groupes of cottages, identical in appearance with the corn-land and the cottages described.

We remember that, coming from a sea-port town, where, to give to property the average security, the usual means had to be resorted to, we were first struck by finding that the door of our relative's cottage, in this inland parish, was furnished with neither lock nor bar. Like that of the hermit in the ballad, it opened with a latch; but, unlike that of the hermit, it was not because there were no stores under the humble roof to demand the care of the master. It was because that, at this comparatively recent period, the crime of theft was unknown in the district. The philosophic Biot, when occupied in measuring the time of the seconds pendulum, resided for several months in one of the smaller Shetland islands; and, fresh from the troubles of France,—his imagination bearing about, if we may so speak, the stains of the guillotine,— the state of trustful security in which he found the simple inhabitants filled him with astonishment. "Here," he exclaimed, "during the twenty-five years in which Europe has been devouring herself, the door of the house I inhabit has remained open day and night." The whole interior of Sutherland was, at the time of which we write, in a similar condition. It did not surprise us that the old man, a person of deep piety, regularly assembled his household night and morning for the purposes of family worship, and led in their devotions: we had seen many such instances in the low country. But it did somewhat surprise us to find the practice universal in the parish. In every family had the worship of God been set up. One could not pass an inhabited cottage in the evening, from which the voice of psalms was not to be heard. On Sabbath morning, the whole population might be seen wending their way, attired in their best, along the blind half-green paths in the heath, to the parish church. The minister was greatly beloved, and all attended his ministrations. We still remember the intense joy which his visits used to impart to the household of our relative. This worthy clergyman still lives, though the infirmities of a stage of life very advanced have gathered round him ; and at the late disruption, choosing his side, and little heeding, when duty called, that his strength had been wasted in the labour of forty years, and that he could now do little more than testify and suffer in behalf of his principles, he resigned his hold of the temporalities as minister of Dornoch, and cast in his lot with his brethren of the Free Church. And his venerable successor in Lairg, a man equally beloved and exemplary, and now on the verge of his eightieth year, has acted a similar part. Had such sacrifices been made in such circumstances for other than the cause of Christ,—had they been made under some such romantic delusion as misled of old the followers of the Stuarts,—the world would have appreciated them highly ; but there is an element in evangelism which repels admiration, unless it be an admiration grounded in faith and love ; and the appeal in such cases must lie, therefore, not to the justice of the world, but to the judgment-seat of God. We may remind the reader, in the passing, that it was the venerable minister of Lairg who, on quitting his manse on the disruption, was received by his widowed daughter into a cottage held of the Duke of Sutherland, and that for this grave crime,—the crime of sheltering her aged father,—the daughter was threatened with ejection by one of the Duke's creatures. Is it not somewhat necessary that the breath of public opinion should be let in on this remote county ? But we digress.

A peculiar stillness seemed to rest over this Highland parish on the Sabbath. The family devotions of the morning, the journey to and from church, and the public services there, occupied fully two-thirds of the day. But there remained the evening, and of it the earlier part was spent in what are known in the north country as fellowship meetings. One of these held regularly in the " ha' " of our relative. From fifteen to twenty people, inclusive of the family, met for the purposes of social prayer and religious conversation, and the time passed profitably away, till the closing night summoned the members of the meeting to their respective homes and their family duties. We marked an interesting peculiarity in the devotions of our relative. He was, as we have said, an old man, and had worshipped in his family long ere Dr Stewart's Gaelic translation of the Scriptures had been introduced into the county ; and as he was supplied in those days with only the English Bible, while his domestics understood only Gaelic, he had to acquire the art, not uncommon in Sutherland at the time, of translating the English chapter for them, as he read, into their native tongue ; and this he had learned to do with such ready fluency, that no one could have guessed it to be other than a Gaelic work from which he was reading. It might have been supposed, however, that the introduction of Dr Stewart's edition would have rendered this mode of translation obsolete ; but in this, and many other families, such was not the case. The old man's Gaelic was *Suther-*

landshire Gaelic. His family understood it better, in consequence, than any other; and so he continued to translate from his English Bible, *ad aperturam libri,* many years after the Gaelic edition had been spread over the county. The fact that such a practice should have been common in Sutherland, says something surely for the intelligence of the family patriarchs of the district. That thousands of the people who knew the Scriptures through no other medium, should have been intimately acquainted with the saving doctrines, and witnesses of their power (and there can be no question that such was the case), is proof enough, at least, that it was a practice carried on with a due perception of the scope and meaning of the sacred volume. One is too apt to associate intelligence with the external improvements of a country,—with well-enclosed fields and white-washed cottages; but the association is altogether a false one. As shown by the testimony of General Stewart of Garth, the Sutherland regiment was not only the most eminently moral, but, as their tastes and habits demonstrated, one of the most decidedly intellectual under the British Crown. Our relative's cottage had, as we have said, its book-case, and both his sons were very intelligent men: but intelligence derived directly from books was not general in the county; a very considerable portion of the people understood no other language than Gaelic, and many of them could not even read; for at this period about one-tenth of the families of Sutherland were distant five or more miles from the nearest school. Their characteristic intelligence was of a kind otherwise derived: it was an intelligence drawn from these domestic readings of the Scriptures, and from the pulpit; and is referred mainly to that profound science which even a Newton could recognise as more important and wonderful than any of the others, but which many of the shallower intellects of our own times deem no science at all. It was an intelligence out of which their morality sprung; it was an intelligence founded in earnest belief.

But what, asks the reader, was the economic condition,—the condition with regard to circumstances and means of living,—of these Sutherland Highlanders? How did they fare? The question has been variously answered: much must depend on the class selected from among them as specimens of the whole,—much, too, taking for granted the honesty of the party who replies, on his own condition in life, and his acquaintance with the circumstances of the poorer people of Scotland generally. The county had its less genial localities, in which, for a month or two in the summer season, when the stock of grain from the previous year was fast running out, and the crops on the ground not yet ripened for use, the people experienced a considerable degree of scarcity,—such scarcity as a mechanic in the south feels when he has been a fortnight out of employment. But the Highlander had resources in these seasons which the mechanic has not. He had his cattle and his wild pot-herbs, such as the mug-wort and the nettle. It has been adduced by the advocates of the change which has ruined Sutherland, as a proof of the extreme hardship of the Highlander's condition, that at such times he could have eaten as food a broth made of nettles, mixed up with a little oatmeal, or have had recourse to the expedient of bleeding his cattle, and making the blood into a sort of pudding. And it is quite true that the Sutherlandshire Highlander was in the habit, at such times, of having recourse to such food. It is not less true, however, that the statement is just as little conclusive regarding his condition, as if it were alleged there must always be famine in France when the people eat the hind legs of frogs, or in Italy when they make dishes of snails. We never saw scarcity in the house of our relative, but we have seen the nettle broth in it very frequently, and the blood-pudding oftener than once; for both dishes were especial favourites with the Highlanders. With regard to the general comfort of the people in their old condition, there are better tests than can be drawn from the kind of food they occasionally ate. The country hears often of dearth in Sutherland now,—every year in which the crop falls a little below average in other districts, is a year of famine there; but the country never heard of dearth in Sutherland then. There were very few among the holders of its small inland farms who had not saved a little money. Their circumstances were such, that their moral nature found full room to develope itself, and in a way the world has rarely witnessed. Never were there a happier or more contented people, or a people more strongly attached to the soil; and not one of them now lives in the altered circumstances on which they were so rudely precipitated by the landlord, who does not look back on this period of comfort and enjoyment with sad and hopeless regret. We have never heard the system which has depopulated this portion of the country defended, without recurring to our two several visits to the turf cottage in Lairg, or without feeling that the defence embodied an essential falsehood, which time will not fail to render evident to the apprehensions of all.

We would but fatigue our readers were we to run over half our recollections of the interior of Sutherland. They are not all of a serious cast. We have sat in the long autumn evenings in the cheerful circle round the turf-fire of the ha', and have heard many a tradition of old clan feuds pleasingly told, and many a song of the poet of the county, Old Rob Donn, gaily sung. In our immediate neighbourhood, by the side of a small stream,—small, but not without its supply of brown trout, speckled with crimson,—there was a spot of green meadow-land, on which the young men of the neighbourhood used not unfrequently to meet and try their vigour in throwing the stone. The stone itself had its history. It was a ball of gneiss, round as a bullet, that had once surmounted the gable of a small Popish chapel, of which there now remained only a shapeless heap of stones, that scarce overtopped the long grass amid which it lay. A few undressed flags indicated an ancient burying-ground; and over the ruined heap, and the rude tomb-stones that told no story, an ancient time-hollowed tree, coeval with the perished building, stretched out its giant arms. Even the sterner occupations of the farm had in their very variety a strong smack of enjoyment. We found one of the old man's sons engaged, during our one visit, in building an out-house, after the primitive fashion of the Highlands, and during our other visit, in constructing a plough. The two main *cupples* of the building he made of huge trees, dug out of a neighbouring morass: they resembled somewhat the beams of a large sloop reversed. The stones he carried from the outfield heath on a sledge; the interstices in the walls he caulked with moss; the roof he covered with sods. The entire erection was his workmanship, from foundation to ridge. And such, in brief, was the history of all those cottages in the interior of Sutherland, which the poor Highlanders so naturally deemed their own, but from which, when set on fire and burnt to the ground by the creatures of the proprietor, they were glad to escape with their lives. The plough, with the exception of the iron work, was altogether our relative's workmanship too. And such was the history of the rude implements of rural or domestic labour which were consumed in the burning dwellings. But we anticipate.

There is little of gaiety or enjoyment among the Highlanders of Sutherland now. We spent a considerable time for two several years among their thickly-clustered cottages on the eastern coast, and saw how they live, and how it happens that when years of comparative scarcity come on they starve. Most of them saved, when in the interior, as we have said, a little money; but the process has been reversed here: in every instance in which they brought their savings to the coast-side has the fund been dissipated. Each cottage has from half an acre to an acre-and-half of corn-land attached to it,—just such patches as the Irish starve upon. In some places, by dint of sore labour, the soil has been considerably improved; and all that seems necessary to render it worth the care of a family, would be just to increase its area some ten or twelve times. In other cases, however, increase would be no advantage. We find it composed of a loose debris of granitic water-rolled pebbles and ferruginous sand, that seem destined to perpetual barrenness. The rents, in every instance, seem moderate: the money of the tenant flows towards the landlord in a stream of not half the volume of that in which the money of the landlord must flow towards the tenant when the poor-laws shall be extended to Scotland. But no rent, in such circumstances, can be really moderate. A clergyman, when asked to say how many of his parishioners, in one of these coast districts, realized *less* than sixpence a-day, replied, that it would be a much easier matter for him to point out how many of them realized *more* than sixpence, as this more fortunate class were exceedingly few. And surely no rent can be moderate that is paid by a man who realizes less than sixpence a-day. It is the peculiar evil produced by the change in Sutherland, that it has consigned the population of the country to a condition in which no rent *can* be moderate,—to a condition in which they but barely avoid famine, when matters are at the best with them, and fall into it in every instance in which the herring fishing, their main and most precarious stay, partially fails, or their crops are just a little more than usually scanty. They are in such a state, that their very means of living are sources, not of comfort, but of distress to them. When the fishing and their crops are comparatively abundant, they live on the bleak edge of want; while failure in either plunges them into a state of intense suffering. And well are these Highlanders aware of the true character of the revolution to which they have been subjected. Our Poor Law Commissioners may find, in this land of growing pauperism, thousands as poor as the people of Sutherland; but they will find no class of the population who can so directly contrast their present destitution with a state of comparative plenty and enjoyment, or who, in consequence of possessing this sad ability, are so deeply embued with a too well-grounded and natural discontent.

But we have not yet said how this ruinous revolution was effected in Sutherland,—how the aggravations of the *mode*, if we may so speak, still fester in the recollections of the people,—or how thoroughly that policy of the lord of the soil, through which he now seems determined to complete the work of ruin which his predecessor began, harmonizes with its worst details. We must first relate, however, a disastrous change which took place, in the providence of God, in the noble family of Sutherland, and which, though it dates fully eighty years back, may be regarded as pregnant with the disasters which afterwards befell the county.

CHAPTER IV.

Such of our readers as are acquainted with the memoir of Lady Glenorchy, must remember a deeply melancholy incident which occurred in the history of this excellent woman, in connection with the noble family of Sutherland. Her only sister had been married to William, seventeenth Earl of Sutherland,—" the last of the good Earls;" " a nobleman," says the Rev. Dr Jones, in his Memoir, " who to the finest person united all the dignity and amenity of manners and character which give lustre to greatness." But his sun was destined soon to go down. Five years after his marriage, which proved one of the happiest, and was blessed with two children, the elder of the two, the young Lady Catherine, a singularly engaging child, was taken from him by death, in his old hereditary castle of Dunrobin. The event deeply affected both parents, and preyed on their health and spirits. It had taken place amid the gloom of a severe northern winter, and in the solitude of the Highlands; and, acquiescing in the advice of friends, the Earl and his lady quitted the family seat, where there was so much to remind them of their bereavement, and sought relief in the more cheerful atmosphere of Bath. But they were not to find it there. Shortly after their arrival, the Earl was seized by a malignant fever, with which, upheld by a powerful constitution, he struggled for fifty-four days, and then expired. " For the first twenty-one days and nights of these," says Dr Jones, " Lady Sutherland never left his bed-side; and then at last, overcome with fatigue, anxiety, and grief, she sank an unavailing victim to an amiable but excessive attachment, seventeen days before the death of her lord." The period, though not very remote, was one in which the intelligence of events travelled slowly; and in this instance the distraction of the family must have served to retard it beyond the ordinary time. Her Ladyship's mother, when hastening from Edinburgh to her assistance, alighted one day from her carriage at an inn, and, on seeing two hearses standing by the way side, inquired of an attendant whose remains they contained? The remains, was the reply, of Lord and Lady Sutherland, on their way for interment to the Royal Chapel of Holyrood House. And such was the first intimation which the lady received of the death of her daughter and son-in-law.

The event was pregnant with disaster to Sutherland, though many years elapsed ere the ruin which it involved fell on that hapless county. The sole survivor and heir of the family was a female infant of but a year old. Her maternal grandmother, an ambitious, intriguing woman of the world, had the chief share in her general training and education; and she was brought up in the south of Scotland, of which her grand-

B

mother was a native, far removed from the influence of those genial sympathies with the people of her clan, for which the old lords of Sutherland had been so remarkable, and, what was a sorer evil still, from the influence of the vitalities of that religion which, for five generations together, her fathers had illustrated and adorned. The special mode in which the disaster told first, was through the patronages of the county, the larger part of which are vested in the family of Sutherland. Some of the old Earls had been content, as we have seen, to place themselves on the level of the Christian men of their parishes, and thus to unite with them in calling to their churches the Christian ministers of their choice. They knew,—what regenerate natures can alone know, with the proper emphasis,—that in Christ Jesus the vassal ranks with his lord, and they conscientiously acted on the conviction. But matters were now regulated differently. The presentation supplanted the call, and ministers came to be placed in the parishes of Sutherland without the consent, and contrary to the will, of the people. Churches, well filled hitherto, were deserted by their congregations, just because a respectable woman of the world, making free use of what she deemed her own, had planted them with men of the world who were only tolerably respectable; and in houses and barns, the devout men of the district learned to hold numerously-attended Sabbath meetings for reading the Scriptures, and mutual exhortation, and prayer, as a sort of substitutes for the public services, in which they found they could no longer join with profit. The spirit awakened by the old Earls had survived themselves, and ran directly counter to the policy of their descendant. Strongly attached to the Establishment, the people, though they thus forsook their old places of worship, still remained members of the national Church, and travelled far in the summer season to attend the better ministers of their own and the neighbouring counties. We have been assured, too, from men whose judgment we respect, that, under all their disadvantages, religion continued peculiarly to flourish among them;—a deep-toned evangelism prevailed; so that perhaps the visible Church throughout the world at the time could furnish no more striking contrast than that which obtained between the cold, bald, common-place services of the pulpit in some of these parishes, and the fervid prayers and exhortations which gave life and interest to these humble meetings of the people. What a pity it is that differences such as these the Duke of Sutherland cannot see!

The marriage of the young countess into a noble English family was fraught with farther disaster to the county. There are many Englishmen quite intelligent enough to perceive the difference between a smoky cottage of turf and a white-washed cottage of stone, whose judgment on their respective inhabitants would be of but little value. Sutherland, as a country of *men*, stood higher at this period than perhaps any other district in the British empire; but, as our descriptions in the preceding chapter must have shown,—and we indulged in them mainly with a view to this part of our subject,—it by no means stood high as a country of farms and cottages. The marriage of the Countess brought a new set of eyes upon it,—eyes accustomed to quite a different face of things. It seemed a wild, rude country, where all was wrong, and all had to be set right,—a sort of Russia on a small scale, that had just got another Peter the Great to civilize it,—or a sort of barbarous Egypt, with an energetic Ali Pasha at its head. Even the vast wealth and great liberality of the Stafford family militated against this hapless county : it enabled them to treat it as the mere subject of an interesting experiment, in which gain to themselves was really no object,—nearly as little so as if they had resolved on dissecting a dog alive for the benefit of science. It was a still further disadvantage, that they had to carry on their experiment by the hands, and to watch its first effects with the eyes, of others. The agonies of the dog might have had their softening influence on a dissecter who held the knife himself ; but there could be no such influence exerted over him, did he merely issue orders to his footman that the dissection should be completed, remaining himself, meanwhile, out of sight and out of hearing. The plan of improvement sketched out by this English family was a plan exceedingly easy of conception. Here is a vast tract of land, furnished with two distinct sources of wealth. Its shores may be made the seats of extensive fisheries, and the whole of its interior parcelled out into productive sheep-farms. All is waste in its present state : it has no fisheries, and two-thirds of its internal produce is consumed by the inhabitants. It had contributed, for the use of the community and the landlord, its large herds of black cattle ; but the English family saw, and, we believe, saw truly, that for every one pound of beef which it produced, it could be made to produce two pounds of mutton, and perhaps a pound of fish in addition. And it was resolved, therefore, that the inhabitants of the central districts, who, *as they were mere Celts*, could not be transformed, it was held, into store-farmers, should be marched down to the sea-side, there to convert themselves into fishermen, on the shortest possible notice, and that a few farmers of capital, of the industrious Lowland race, should be invited to occupy the new subdivisions of the interior.

And, pray, what objections can be urged against so liberal and large-minded a scheme? The poor inhabitants of the interior had *very* serious objections to urge against it. Their humble dwellings were of their own rearing ; it was they themselves who had broken in their little fields from the waste ; from time immemorial, far beyond the reach of history, had they possessed their mountain holdings,—they had defended them so well of old, that the soil was still virgin ground, in which the invader had found only a grave ; and their young men were now in foreign lands, fighting, at the command of their chieftainess, the battles of their country, not in the character of hired soldiers, but of men who regarded these very holdings as their stake in the quarrel. To them, then, the scheme seemed fraught with the most flagrant, the most monstrous injustice. Were it to be suggested by some Chartist convention in a time of revolution, that Sutherland might be still further improved,—that it was really a piece of great waste to suffer the revenues of so extensive a district to be squandered by one individual,—that it would be better to appropriate them to the use of the community in general,—that the community in general might be still further benefited by the removal of the one said individual from Dunrobin to a road-side, where he might be profitably employed in breaking stones,—and that this new arrangement could not be entered on too soon,—the noble Duke would not be a whit more astonished, or rendered a whit more indignant, by the scheme, than were the Highlanders of Sutherland by the scheme of his predecessor.

The reader must keep in view, therefore, that if atrocities unexampled in Britain for at least a century were perpetrated in the *clearing of*

Sutherland, there was a species of at least passive resistance on the part of the people (for active resistance there was none), which in some degree provoked them. Had the Highlanders, on receiving orders, marched down to the sea-coast, and become fishermen, with the readiness with which a regiment deploys on review day, the atrocities would, we doubt not, have been much fewer. But though the orders were very distinct, the Highlanders were very unwilling to obey; and the severities formed merely a part of the means through which the necessary obedience was ultimately secured. We shall instance a single case, as illustrative of the process. In the month of March 1814, a large proportion of the Highlanders of Farr and Kildonan, two parishes in Sutherland, were summoned to quit their farms in the following May. In a few days after, the surrounding heaths on which they pastured their cattle, and from which at that season the sole supply of herbage is derived (for in those northern districts the grass springs late, and the cattle-feeder in the spring months depends chiefly on the heather), were set on fire and burnt up. There was that sort of policy in the stroke which men deem allowable in a state of war. The starving cattle went roaming over the burnt pastures, and found nothing to eat. Many of them perished, and the greater part of what remained, though in miserable condition, the Highlanders had to sell perforce. Most of the able-bodied men were engaged in this latter business at a distance from home, when the dreaded term-day came on. The pasturage had been destroyed before the legal term, and while, in even the eye of the law, it was still the property of the poor Highlanders; but ere disturbing them in their dwellings, term-day was suffered to pass. The work of demolition then began. A numerous party of men, with a factor at their head, entered the district, and commenced pulling down the houses over the heads of the inhabitants. In an extensive tract of country not a human dwelling was left standing, and then, the more effectually to prevent their temporary re-erection, the destroyers set fire to the wreck. In one day were the people deprived of home and shelter, and left exposed to the elements. Many deaths are said to have ensued from alarm, fatigue, and cold. Pregnant women were taken with premature labour in the open air. There were old men who took to the woods and rocks in a state of partial insanity. An aged bedridden man, named Macbeath, had his house unroofed over his head, and was left exposed to wind and rain till death put a period to his sufferings. Another man lying ill of a fever met with no tenderer treatment, but in his case the die turned up life. A bedridden woman, nearly a hundred years of age, had her house fired over her head, and ere she could be extricated from the burning wreck, the sheets in which she was carried were on fire. She survived but for five days after. In a critique on the work of Sismondi, which appeared a few months since in the *Westminster Review*, the writer tells us, " it has even been said that an old man, having refused to quit his cabin, perished in the flames." But such was not the case. The constituted authorities interfered; a precognition was taken by the Sheriff-Substitute of the county, and the case tried before the Justiciary Court at Inverness; but the trial terminated in the acquittal of the pannels. There was no punishable crime proven to attach to the agents of the proprietor.

Their acquittal was followed by scenes of a similar character with the scene described, and of even greater atrocity. But we must borrow the description of one of these from the historian of the *clearing* of Sutherland,—Donald M'Leod, a native of the county, and himself a sufferer in the experimental process to which it was subjected :—

"The work of devastation was begun by setting fire to the houses of the small tenants in extensive districts,—Farr, Rogart, Golspie, and the whole parish of Kildonan. I was an eye-witness of the scene. The calamity came on the people quite unexpectedly. Strong parties for each district, furnished with faggots and other combustibles, rushed on the dwellings of the devoted people, and immediately commenced setting fire to them, proceeding in their work with the greatest rapidity, till about three hundred houses were in flames. Little or no time was given for the removal of persons or property,—the consternation and confusion were extreme,—the people striving to remove the sick and the helpless before the fire should reach them,—next struggling to save the most valuable of their effects,—the cries of the women and children,—the roaring of the affrighted cattle, hunted by the dogs of the shepherds amid the smoke and the fire,—altogether composed a scene that completely baffles description. A dense cloud of smoke enveloped the whole country by day, and even extended far on the sea. At night, an awfully grand but terrific scene presented itself,—all the houses in an extensive district in flames at once. I myself ascended a height about eleven o'clock in the evening, and counted two hundred and fifty blazing houses, many of the owners of which were my relations, and all of whom I personally knew, but whose present condition I could not tell. The conflagration lasted six days, till the whole of the dwellings were reduced to ashes or smoking ruins. During one of these days, a boat lost her way in the dense smoke as she approached the shore, but at night she was enabled to reach a landing place by the light of the flames."

But, to employ the language of Southey,

> "Things such as these, we know, must be
> At every famous victory."

And in this instance the victory of the lord of the soil over the children of the soil was signal and complete. In little more than nine years a population of fifteen thousand individuals were removed from the interior of Sutherland to its sea-coasts, or had emigrated to America. The inland districts were converted into deserts, through which the traveller may take a long day's journey, amid ruins that still bear the scathe of fire, and grassy patches betraying, when the evening sun casts aslant its long deep shadows, the half-effaced lines of the plough. The writer of the singularly-striking passage we have just quoted, revisited his native place (Kildonan) in the year 1828, and attended divine service in the parish church. A numerous and devout congregation had once worshipped there : the congregation now consisted of eight shepherds and their *dogs*. In a neighbouring district,—the barony of Strathnaver, a portion of the parish of Farr,—the church, no longer found necessary, was razed to the ground. The timber was carried away to be used in the erection of an inn, and the minister's house converted into the dwelling of a fox-hunter. "A woman well known in the parish," says M'Leod, "happening to traverse the Strath the year after the burning, was asked, on her return, what news? 'Oh,' said she, '*sgeul bronach, sgeul bronach!* sad news, sad news! I have seen the timber of our kirk covering the inn at Altnaharran; I have seen the kirkyard, where our friends are mouldering, filled with tarry sheep, and Mr Sage's study-room a kennel for Robert Gun's dogs.'"

CHAPTER V.

LET us follow, for a little, the poor Highlanders of Sutherland to the sea-coast. It would be easy dwelling on the terrors of their expulsion, and multiplying facts of horror; but had there been no permanent deterioration effected in their condition, these, all harrowing and repulsive as they were, would have mattered less. Sutherland would have soon recovered the burning up of a few hundred hamlets, or the loss of a few bed-ridden old people, who would have died as certainly under cover, though perhaps a few months later, as when exposed to the elements in the open air. Nay, had it lost a thousand of its best men in the way in which it lost so many at the storming of New Orleans, the blank ere now would have been completely filled up. The calamities of fire or of decimation even, however distressing in themselves, never yet ruined a country: no calamity ruins a country that leaves the surviving inhabitants to develop, in their old circumstances, their old character and resources.

In one of the eastern eclogues of Collins, where two shepherds are described as flying for their lives before the troops of a ruthless invader, we see with how much of the terrible the imagination of a poet could invest the evils of war, when aggravated by pitiless barbarity. Fertile as that imagination was, however, there might be found new circumstances to heighten the horrors of the scene,—circumstances beyond the reach of invention,—in the retreat of the Sutherland Highlanders from the smoking ruins of their cottages to their allotments on the coast. We have heard of one man, named M'Kay, whose family, at the time of the greater conflagration referred to by M'Leod, were all lying ill of fever, who had to carry two of his sick children on his back a distance of twenty-five miles. We have heard of the famished people blackening the shores, like the crew of some vessel wrecked on an inhospitable coast, that they might sustain life by the shell-fish and sea-weed laid bare by the ebb. Many of their allotments, especially on the western coast, were barren in the extreme,—unsheltered by bush or tree, and exposed to the sweeping sea-winds, and, in time of tempest, to the blighting spray; and it was found a matter of the extremest difficulty to keep the few cattle which they had retained, from wandering, especially in the night-time, into the better sheltered and more fertile interior. The poor animals were intelligent enough to read a practical comment on the nature of the change effected; and, from the harshness of the shepherds to whom the care of the interior had been entrusted, they served materially to add to the distress of their unhappy masters. They were getting continually impounded; and vexatious fines, in the form of trespass-money, came thus to be wrung from the already impoverished Highlanders. Many who had no money to give were obliged to relieve them by depositing some of their few portable articles of value, such as bed or body clothes, or, more distressing still, watches, and rings, and pins,—the only relics, in not a few instances, of brave men whose bones were mouldering under the fatal rampart at New Orleans, or in the arid sands of Egypt,—on that spot of proud recollection, where the invincibles of Napoleon went down before the Highland bayonet. Their first efforts as fishermen were what might be expected from a rural people unaccustomed to the sea. The shores of

Sutherland for immense tracts together, are iron-bound, and much exposed,—open on the eastern coast to the waves of the German Ocean, and on the north and west to the long roll of the Atlantic. There could not be more perilous seas for the unpractised boatman to take his first lessons on ; but though the casualties were numerous, and the loss of life great, many of the younger Highlanders became expert fishermen. The experiment was harsh in the extreme, but so far, at least, it succeeded. It lies open, however, to other objections than those which have been urged against it on the score of its inhumanity.

The reader must be acquainted with Goldsmith's remarks on the herring fishery of his days. " A few years ago," he says, " the herring fishing employed all Grub Street ; it was the topic in every coffee-house, and the burden of every ballad. We were to drag up oceans of gold from the bottom of the sea ; we were to supply all Europe with herrings upon our own terms. At present, however, we hear no more of all this ; we have fished up very little gold that I can learn ; nor do we furnish the world with herrings, as was expected." We have, in this brief passage, a history of all the more sanguine expectations which have been founded on herring fisheries. There is no branch of industry so calculated to awaken the hopes of the speculator, or so suited to disappoint them. So entirely is this the case, that were we desirous to reduce an industrious people to the lowest stage of wretchedness compatible with industry, we would remove them to some barren district, and there throw them on the resources of this fishery exclusively. The employments of the herring fisher have all the uncertainty of the ventures of the gambler. He has first to lay down, if we may so speak, a considerable stake,—for his drift of nets and his boat involve a very considerable outlay of capital ; and, if successful, and if in general the fishery be *not* successful, the *take* of a single week may more than remunerate him. A single cast of his nets may bring him in thirty guineas and more. The die turns up in his favour, and he sweeps the board. And hence those golden dreams of the speculator, so happily described by Goldsmith. But year after year may pass, and the run of luck be against the fisherman. A fishing generally good at all the stations gluts the market, necessarily limited in its demands to an average supply, and, from the bulk and weight of the commodity, not easily extended to distant parts ; and the herring merchant first, and the fisherman next, find that they have been labouring hard to little purpose. Again, a fishing under average, from the eccentric character of the fish, is found almost always to benefit a few, and to ruin a great many. The average deficiency is never equally spread over the fishermen ; one sweeps the board,—another loses all. Nor are the cases few in which the accustomed shoal wholly deserts a tract of coast for years together ; and thus the lottery, precarious at all times, becomes a lottery in which there are only blanks to be drawn. The wealthy speculator might perhaps watch such changes, and, by supplementing the deficiency of one year by the abundance of another, give to the whole a character of average ; but, alas for the poor labouring man placed in such circumstances ! The yearly disbursements of our Scottish Fishery Board, in the way of assistance to poverty-struck fishermen, unable even to repair their boats, testify all too tangibly that they cannot regulate their long runs of ill luck by their temporary successes ! And if such be the case among our hereditary fishermen of the north, who derive more than half their sustenance from the white fishery, how much more must it affect those fishermen of Sutherland, who, having no market for their white fish in the depopulated interior, and no merchants settled among them to find markets farther away, have to depend exclusively on their herring fishing. The experiment which precipitated the population of the country on its barer skirts, as some diseases precipitate the humours on the extremities, would have been emphatically a disastrous one, so far at least as the people were concerned, even did it involve no large amount of human suffering, and no deterioration of character.

One of the first writers, of unquestioned respectability, who acquainted the public with the true character of the revolution which had been effected in Sutherland, was the late General Stewart of Garth. He was, we believe, the first man,—and the fact says something for his shrewdness, —who saw a coming poor-law looming through the *clearing* of Sutherland. His statements are exceedingly valuable,—his inferences almost always just. The General,—a man of probity and nice honour,—had such an ability of estimating the value of moral excellence in a people, as the originators of the revolution had of estimating the antagonist merits of double pounds of mutton and single pounds of beef. He had seen printed representations on the subject,—tissues of hollow falsehood, that have since been repeated in newspapers and reviews; and though unacquainted with the facts at the time, he saw sufficient reason to question their general correctness, from the circumstance that he found in them the character of the people, with which no man could be better acquainted, vilified and traduced. The General saw one leviathan falsehood running through the whole, and, on the strength of the old adage, naturally suspected the company in which he found it. And so, making minute and faithful inquiry, he published the results at which he arrived. He refers to the mode of ejectment by the torch. He next goes on to show how some of the ejected tenants were allowed small allotments of moor on the coast side, of from half an acre to two acres in extent, which it was their task to break into corn-land; and how that, because many patches of green appear in this way, where all was russet before, the change has been much eulogized as improvement. We find him remarking further, with considerable point and shrewdness, that, " many persons are, however, inclined to doubt the advantages of improvements which call for such frequent apologies," and that, " if the advantage to the people were so evident, or if more lenient measures had been pursued, vindication could not have been necessary." The General knew how to pass from the green spots themselves, to the condition of those who tilled them. The following passage must strike all acquainted with the Highlanders of Sutherland as a true representation of the circumstances to which they have been reduced :—

" Ancient respectable tenants who have passed the greater part of life in the enjoyment of abundance, and in the exercise of hospitality and charity, possessing stock of ten, twenty, and thirty breeding cows, with the usual proportion of other stock, are now pining on one or two acres of bad land, with one or two starved cows, and for this accommodation a calculation is made, that they must support their families, and pay the rent of their lots, not from the produce, but from the sea; thus drawing a rent which the land cannot afford ! When the herring fishing succeeds, they generally satisfy the landlord, whatever privations they may suffer ; but when the fishing fails, they fall into arrears. The herring fishing, always precarious, has for a succession of years been very defective, and this class of people are reduced to extreme misery. At first, some of them possessed capital, from converting their farm-stock into cash, but this has been long exhausted ; and it is truly distressing to view their general poverty, aggravated by their having once enjoyed abundance and independence."

Some of the removals to which we have referred took place during that group of scarce seasons in which the year 1816 was so prominent; but the scarcity which these induced served merely to render the other sufferings of the people more intense, and was lost sight of in the general extent of the calamity. Another group of hard seasons came on,—one of those groupes which seem of such certain, and yet of such irregular occurrence in our climate, that though they have attracted notice from the days of Bacon downwards, they have hitherto resisted all attempts to include them in some definite cycle. The summer and harvest of 1835 were the last of a series of fine summers and abundant harvests ; and for six years after, there was less than the usual heat, and more than the usual rain. Science, in connection with agriculture, has done much for us in the low country; and so our humbler population were saved from the horrors of a dearth of food ; but on the green patches which girdle the shores of Sutherland, and which have been esteemed such wonderful improvements, science had done and could do nothing. The people had been sinking lower and lower during the previous twenty years, and what would have been great hardship before had became famine now. One feels at times that it may be an advantage to have lived among the humbler people. We have been enabled, in consequence, to detect many such gross mis-statements as those with which the apologists of the disastrous revolution effected in Sutherland have attempted to gloss over the ruin of that country. In other parts of the Highlands, especially in the Hebrides, the failure of the kelp trade did much to impoverish the inhabitants ; but in the Highlands of Sutherland the famine was the effect of *improvement* alone.

The writer of these chapters saw how a late, untoward year operates on the bleak shores of the north-western Highlands, when spending a season there a good many years ago. He found what only a few twelve-months previous had been a piece of dark moor, laid out into minute patches of corn, and bearing a dense population. The herring fishing had failed for the two seasons before, and the poor cottars were, in consequence, in arrears with their rent; but the crops had been tolerable ; and though their stores of meal and potatoes were all exhausted at the time of our coming among them (the month of June), and though no part of the growing crop was yet fit for use, the white fishing was abundant, and a training of hardship had enabled them to subsist on fish exclusively. Their corn shot in the genial sunshine, and gave fair promise ; and their potatoes had become far enough advanced to supplement their all too meagre meals, when, after a terrible thunder storm, the fine weather broke up, and for thirteen weeks together there scarce passed a day without its baffling winds and its heavy chilling showers. The oats withered without ripening,—the hardy bear might be seen rustling on all the more exposed slopes, light as the common rye-grass of our hay fields, the stalks, in vast proportion, shorn of the ears. It was only in a very few of the more sheltered places that it yielded a scanty return of a dark-coloured and shrivelled grain. And to impart a still deeper shade to the prospects of the poor Highlanders, the herring fishery failed as signally as in the previous years. There awaited them all too obviously a whole half year of inevitable famine, unless Lowland charity interfered in their behalf. And the recurrence of this state of things no amount of providence or exertion on their own part, when placed in such circumstances, can obviate or prevent. It was a conviction of this character, based on experience, which led the writer of these remarks to state, when giving evidence before the present Poor Law Commissioners for Scotland, that though opposed to the principle of legal assessment generally, he could yet see no other mode of reaching the destitution of the Highlands. Our humane Scottish law compels the man who sends another man to prison to support him there, just because it is held impossible that within the walls of a prison a man can support himself. Should the principle alter, if, instead of sending him to a prison, he banishes him to a bleak, inhospitable coast, where, unless he receives occasional support from others, he must inevitably perish?

The sufferings of the people of Sutherland during the first of these years of destitution (1836), we find strikingly described by M'Leod :—

" In this year," says the author, " the crops all over Britain were deficient, having bad weather for growing and ripening, and still worse for gathering in. But in the Highlands, they were an entire failure, and on the untoward spots, occupied by the Sutherland small tenants, there was literally nothing fit for human subsistence. And to add to the calamity, the weather had prevented them from securing the peats, their only fuel, so that to their previous state of exhaustion, cold and hunger were to be superadded. The sufferings endured by the poor Highlanders in the succeeding winter truly beggar description. Even the herring fishing had failed, and consequently their credit in Caithness, which depended on its success, was at an end. Any little provision they might be able to procure was of the most inferior and unwholesome description. It was no uncommon thing to see people searching among the snow for the frosted potatoes to eat, in order to preserve life. As the harvest had been disastrous, so the winter was uncommonly boisterous and severe, and consequently little could be obtained from the sea to mitigate the calamity. The distress rose to such a height as to cause a sensation all over the island, and there arose a general cry for Government interference, to save the people from death by famine."

Public meetings were held, private subscriptions entered into, large funds collected, the British people responded to the cry of their suffering fellow-subjects, and relief was extended to every portion of the Highlands except one. Alas for poor Sutherland ! There, it was said, the charity of the country was not required, as the noble and wealthy proprietors had themselves resolved to interfere : and as this statement was circulated extensively through the public prints, and sedulously repeated at all public meetings, the mind of the community was set quite at rest on the matter. And interfere the proprietors at length did. Late in the spring of 1837, after sufferings the most incredible had been endured, and disease and death had been among the wretched people, they received a scanty supply of meal and seed-corn, for which, though vaunted at the time as a piece of munificent charity, the greater part of them had afterwards to pay.

In the next chapter we shall endeavour bringing these facts to bear on the cause of the Free Church in Sutherland. We close for the present by adding just one curious fact more. We have already shown how the bleak moors of Sutherland have been mightily improved by the revolution which ruined its people. They bear many green patches which were brown before. Now, it so happened that rather more than ten years ago, the idea struck the original improvers, that as green was an improvement on brown, so far as the moors were concerned, white would be an equally decided improvement on black, so far as the houses were concerned. An order was accordingly issued, in the name of the Duke and Duchess of Sutherland, that all the small tenants on both sides the public road, where it stretches on the northern coast from the confines of Reay to the Kyle of Tongue, a distance of about thirty miles, should straightway build themselves new houses of stone and mortar, according to a prescribed plan and specification. Pharaoh's famous order could not have bred greater consternation. But the only alternative given was summed up in the magic word *removal;* and the poor Highlanders, dejected, tamed, broken in spirit as in means, well knew from experience what the magic word meant. And so, as their prototypes set themselves to gather stubble for their bricks, the poor Highlanders began to build. We again quote from M'Leod :—

" Previous to this, in the year 1829, I and my family had been forced away, like others, being particularly obnoxious to those in authority for sometimes showing an inclination to oppose their tyranny, and therefore we had to be made examples of to frighten the rest ; but in 1833 I made a tour of the district, when the building was going on, and shall endeavour to describe a small part of what met my eye on that occasion. In one locality (and this was a specimen of the rest) I saw fourteen different squads of masons at work, with the natives attending them. Old grey-headed men, worn down by previous hardship and present want, were to be seen carrying stones, and wheeling them and other materials on barrows, or conveying them on their backs to the buildings, and with their tottering limbs and trembling hands straining to raise them on the walls. The young men also, after toiling all night at sea endeavouring for subsistence, were obliged to yield their exhausted frames to the labours of the day. Even female labour could not be dispensed with ; the strong as well as the weak, the delicate and sickly, and (shame to their oppressors), even the pregnant, bare-footed and scantily clothed, were obliged to join in those rugged, unfeminine labours. In one instance I saw the husband quarrying stones, and the wife and children dragging them along in an old cart to the building. Such were the building scenes of that period. The poor people had often to give the last morsel of food they possessed to feed the masons, and subsist on shellfish themselves. This went on for several years, in the course of which, many hundreds of these houses were erected on unhospitable spots unfit for a human residence."

We add one other extract from the same writer :—

" It might be thought," adds M'Leod, " that the design of forcing the people to build such houses was to provide for their comfort and accommodation, but there seems to have been quite a different object, which, I believe, was the true motive, and that was, to hide the misery that prevailed. There had been a great sensation created in the public mind by the cruelties exercised in these districts ; and it was thought that a number of neat white houses, ranged on each side of the road, would take the eye of strangers and visitors, and give a practical contradiction to the rumours afloat. Hence the poor creatures were forced to resort to such means, and to endure such hardships and privations as I have described, to carry the scheme into effect. And after they had spent their remaining all, and more than their all, on the erection of these houses, and involved themselves in debt, for which they have been harassed and pursued ever since, what are these erections but whitened tombs ; many of them now ten years in existence, and still without proper doors or windows, destitute of furniture and of comfort,—the unhappy lairs of a heart-broken, squalid, fast-degenerating race."

CHAPTER VI.

WE have exhibited to our readers, in the *clearing* of Sutherland, a process of ruin so thoroughly disastrous, that it might be deemed scarce possible to render it more complete. And yet with all its apparent completeness, it admitted of a supplementary process. To employ one of the striking figures of Scripture, it was possible to grind into powder what had been previously broken into fragments,—to degrade the poor inhabitants to a still lower level than that on which they had been so cruelly precipitated,—though persons of a not very original cast of mind might have found it difficult to say how; and the Duke of Sutherland has been ingenious enough to fall on exactly the one proper expedient for supplementing their ruin. All in mere circumstance and situation that could lower and deteriorate, had been present as ingredients in the first process; but there still remained for the people, however reduced to poverty or broken in spirit, all in religion that consoles and ennobles. Sabbath-days came round with their humanizing influences; and, under the teachings of the gospel, the poor and the oppressed looked longingly forward to a future scene of being, in which there is no poverty and no oppression. They still possessed, amid their misery, something positively good, of which it was possible to deprive them; and hence the ability derived to the present lord of Sutherland, of deepening and rendering more signal the ruin accomplished by his predecessor.

Napoleon, when on the eve of re-establishing Popery in France, showed his conviction of the importance of national religions, by remarking that, did there exist no ready-made religion to serve his turn, he would be under the necessity of making one on purpose. And his remark, though perhaps thrown into this form merely to give it point, and render it striking, has been instanced as a proof that he could not have considered the matter very profoundly. It has been said, and said truly, that religions of stamina enough to be even politically useful cannot be *made*,—that it is comparatively easy to gain great battles, and frame important laws; but that to create belief lay beyond the power of even a Napoleon. France, instead of crediting his manufactured religion, would have laughed at both him and it. The Duke of Sutherland has, however, taken upon himself a harder task than the one to which Napoleon could refer, probably in joke. His aim seems to be, not the comparatively simple one of making a new religion where no religion existed before, but of making men already firm in their religious convictions believe that to be a religion which they believe to be no such thing. His undertaking involves a *discharging* as certainly as an *injecting* process,—the erazure of an existing belief, as certainly as the infusion of an antagonist belief that has no existence. We have shown how Evangelism took root and grew in Sutherland, as the only form of Christianity which its people could recognise,—how the antagonist principle of Moderatism they failed to recognise as Christianity at all,—and how, when the latter was obtruded into their pulpits, they withdrew from the churches in which their fathers had worshipped, for they could regard them as churches no longer, and held their prayer and fellowship meetings in their own homes, or travelled far to attend the ministrations of clergymen in whose mission they *could* believe. We have shown that this state of feeling and belief still pervades the county. It led to an actual disruption between its Evangelized people and its Moderate clergy, long ere the disruption of last May took place : that important event has had but the effect of marshalling them into one compact body under a new name. They are adherents of the Free Church now, just because they have been adherents to its principles for the last two centuries. And to shake them loose from this adherence is the object of his Grace,—to reverse the belief of ages,—to render them indifferent to that which they feel and believe to be religion,—and to make them regard as religion that which they know to be none. His task is harder by a great deal than that to which Napoleon barely ventured to advert ; and how very coarse and repulsive his purposed means of accomplishing it !

These harmonize but too well with the mode in which the interior of Sutherland was cleared, and the improved cottages of its sea-coasts erected. The plan has its two items. No sites are to be granted in the district for Free churches, and no dwelling-houses for Free-Church ministers. The climate is severe,—the winters prolonged and stormy,—the roads which connect the chief seats of population with the neighbouring counties, dreary and long. May not ministers and people be eventually worn out in this way ? Such is the portion of the plan which his Grace and his Grace's creatures can afford to present to the light. But there are supplementary items of a somewhat darker kind. The poor cottars are, in the great majority of cases, tenants at will ; and there has been much pains taken to inform them, that to the crime of entertaining and sheltering a Protesting minister, the penalty of ejection from their holdings must inevitably attach. The laws of Charles have again returned in this unhappy district, and free and tolerating Scotland has got, in the nineteenth century, as in the seventeenth, its intercommuned ministers. We shall not say that the intimation has emanated from the Duke. It is the misfortune of such men, that there creep around them creatures whose business it is to anticipate their wishes ; but who, at times, doubtless, instead of anticipating, misinterpret them ; and who, even when not very much mistaken, impart to whatever they do the impress of their own low and menial natures, and thus exaggerate in the act, the intention of their masters. We do not say, therefore, that the intimation has emanated from the Duke ; but this we say, that an exemplary Sutherlandshire minister of the Protesting Church, who resigned his worldly all for the sake of his principles, had lately to travel, that he might preach to his attached people, a long journey of forty-five miles outwards, and as much in return, and all this without taking shelter under the cover of a roof, or without partaking of any other refreshment than that furnished by the slender store of provisions which he had carried with him from his new home. Willingly would the poor Highlanders·have received him at any risk ; but knowing from experience what a Sutherlandshire removal means, he preferred enduring any amount of hardship, rather than that the hospitality of his people should be made the occasion of their ruin. We have already adverted to the case of a lady of Sutherland threatened with ejection from her home because she had extended the shelter of her roof to one of the Protesting clergy, —an aged and venerable man, who had quitted the neighbouring manse, his home for many years, because he could no longer enjoy it in consistency with his principles; and we have shown that that aged and venerable man was the lady's own father. What amount of oppression of a smaller and more petty character may not be expected in the circumstances, when cases such as these are found to stand but a very little over the ordinary level?

The meannesses to which ducal hostility can stoop in this hapless district, impress with a feeling of surprise. In the parish of Dornoch, for instance, where his Grace is fortunately not the sole landowner, there has been a site procured on the most generous terms from Sir George Gun Munro of Poyntzfield; and this gentleman,—believing himself possessed of a hereditary right to a quarry, which, though on the Duke's ground, had been long resorted to by the proprietors of the district generally,—instructed the builder to take from it the stones which he needed. Here, however, his Grace interfered. Never had the quarry been prohibited before; but, on this occasion, a stringent interdict arrested its use. If his Grace could not prevent a hated Free Church from arising in the district, he could at least add to the *expense* of its erection. We have even heard that the portion of the building previously erected had to be pulled down, and the stones returned.

How are we to account for a hostility so determined, and that can stoop so low? In two different ways, we are of opinion, and in both have the people of Scotland a direct interest. Did his Grace entertain a very intense regard for Established Presbytery, it is probable that he himself would be a Presbyterian of the Establishment. But such is not the case. The Church into which he would so fain force the people has been long since deserted by himself. The secret of the course which he pursues can have no connection therefore with religious motive or belief. It can be no proselytising spirit that misleads his Grace. Let us remark, in the first place, rather, however, in the way of embodying a fact than imputing a motive, that with his present views, and in his present circumstances, it may not seem particularly his Grace's interest to make the county of Sutherland a happy or desirable home to the people of Sutherland. It may not seem his Grace's interest that the population of the district should increase. The *clearing* of the sea-coast may seem as little prejudicial to his Grace's welfare now, as the *clearing* of the interior seemed adverse to the interests of his predecessor thirty years ago; nay, it is quite possible that his Grace may be led to regard the *clearing* of the coast as the better and more important *clearing* of the two. Let it not be forgotten that a poor-law hangs over Scotland,— that the shores of Sutherland are covered with what seems one vast straggling village, inhabited by an impoverished and ruined people,— and that the coming assessment may yet fall so weighty, that the extra profits derived to his Grace from his large sheep-farms, may go but a small way in supporting his extra paupers. It is not in the least improbable, that he may live to find the revolution effected by his predecessor taking to itself the form, not of a crime,—for that would be nothing,—but of a disastrous and very terrible blunder.

There is another remark which may prove not unworthy the consideration of the reader. Ever since the completion of the fatal experiment which ruined Sutherland, the noble family through which it was originated and carried on have betrayed the utmost jealousy of having its real results made public. Volumes of special pleading have been written on the subject,—pamphlets have been published,—laboured articles have been inserted in widely-spread reviews,—statistical accounts have been watched over with the most careful surveillance. If the misrepresentations of the press could have altered the matter of fact, famine would not have been gnawing the vitals of Sutherland in every year just a little less abundant than its fellows, nor would the dejected and oppressed people be feeding their discontent, amid present misery, with the recollections of a happier past. If a singularly well-conditioned and wholesome district of country has been converted into one wide ulcer of wretchedness and wo, it must be confessed that the sore has been carefully bandaged up from the public eye,—that if there has been little done for its cure, there has at least been much done for its concealment. Now, be it remembered, that the Free Church threatens to insert a *tent* into this wound, and so keep it open. It has been said that the Gaelic language removes a district more effectually from the influence of English opinion than an ocean of three thousand miles, and that the British public know better what is doing in New York than what is doing in Lewis or Skye. And hence one cause, at least, of the thick obscurity that has so long enveloped the miseries which the poor Highlander has had to endure, and the oppressions to which he has been subjected. The Free Church threatens to *translate* her wrongs into English, and to give them currency in the general mart of opinion. She might possibly enough be no silent spectator of conflagrations such as those which characterized the first general improvement of Sutherland,—nor yet of such Egyptian schemes of house-building as that which formed part of the improvements of a later plan. She might be somewhat apt to betray the real state of the district, and thus render laborious misrepresentation of little avail. She might effect a diversion in the cause of the people, and shake the foundations of the hitherto despotic power which has so long weighed them down. She might do for Sutherland what Cobbett promised to do for it, but what Cobbett had not character enough to accomplish, and what he did not live even to attempt. A combination of circumstances have conspired to vest in a Scottish proprietor, in this northern district, a more despotic power than even the most absolute monarchs of the Continent possess ; and it is, perhaps, no great wonder that that proprietor should be jealous of the introduction of an element which threatens, it may seem, materially to lessen it. And so he struggles hard to exclude the Free Church, and, though no member of the Establishment himself, declaims warmly in its behalf. Certain it is, that from the Establishment, as now constituted, he can have nothing to fear, and the people nothing to hope.

After what manner may his Grace the Duke of Sutherland be most effectually met in this matter, so that the cause of toleration and freedom of conscience may be maintained in the extensive district which

God, in his providence, has consigned to his stewardship? We shall in our next chapter attempt giving the question an answer. Meanwhile, we trust the people of Sutherland will continue, as hitherto, to stand firm. The strong repugnance which they feel against being driven into churches which all their better ministers have left, is not ill founded. No Church of God ever employs such means of conversion as those employed by his Grace: they are means which have been often resorted to for the purpose of making men worse,—never yet for the purpose of making them better. We know that with their long formed church-going habits, the people must feel their now silent Sabbaths pass heavily; but they would perhaps do well to remember, amid the tedium and the gloom, that there were good men who not only anticipated such a time of trial for this country, but who also made provision for it. Thomas Scott, when engaged in writing his Commentary, used to solace himself with the belief that it might be of use at a period when the public worship of God would be no longer tolerated in the land. To the great bulk of the people of Sutherland that time seems to have already come. They know, however, the value of the old divines, and have not a few of their more practical treatises translated into their own expressive tongue,—*Alleine's Alarm,—Boston's Fourfold State,—Doddridge's Rise and Progress,—Baxter's Call,—Guthrie's Saving Interest.* Let these, and such as these, be their preachers, when they can procure no other. The more they learn to relish them, the less will they relish the bald and miserable services of the Residuary Church. Let them hold their fellowship and prayer meetings,—let them keep up the worship of God in their families: the cause of religious freedom in the district is involved in the stand which they make. Above all, let them possess their souls in patience. We are not unacquainted with the Celtic character, as developed in the Highlands of Scotland. Highlanders, up to a certain point, are the most docile, patient, enduring of men; but that point once passed, endurance ceases, and the all too gentle lamb starts up an angry lion. The spirit is stirred that maddens at the sight of the naked weapon, and that, in its headlong rush upon the enemy, discipline can neither check nor control. Let our oppressed Highlanders of Sutherland beware. They have suffered much; but, so far as man is the agent, their battles can be fought on only the arena of public opinion, and on that ground which the political field may be soon found to furnish. Any explosion of violence on their part would be ruin to both the Free Church and themselves.

CHAPTER VII.

How is the battle of religious freedom to be best fought in behalf of the oppressed people of Sutherland? We shall attempt throwing out a few simple suggestions on the subject, which, if in the right tract, the reader may find it easy to follow up and mature.

First, then, let us remember, that in this country, in which opinion is all-potent, and which for at least a century and a half has been the envy of Continental States, for the degree of religious freedom which it enjoys, the policy of the Duke of Sutherland cannot be known without being condemned. The current which he opposes has been scooping out its channel for ages. Every great mind produced by Britain, from the times of Milton and Locke down to the times of Mackintosh and of Chalmers, has been giving it impetus in but one direction; and it is scarce likely that it will reverse its course now, at the bidding of a few intolerant and narrow-minded aristocrats. British opinion has but to be fairly appealed to, in order to declare strongly in favour of the oppressed Highlanders of Sutherland. What we would first remark, then, is, that the policy of his Grace the Duke cannot be too widely exposed. The press and the platform must be employed. The frank and generous English must be told, that that law of religious toleration which did so much at a comparatively early period to elevate the character of their country in the eye of the world, and which, in these latter times, men have been accustomed to regard as somewhat less, after all, than an adequate embodiment of the rights of conscience, has been virtually repealed in a populous and very extensive district of the British empire, through a capricious exercise of power on the part of a single man. Why, it has been asked, in a matter which lies between God and the conscience, and between God and the conscience only, should a third party be permitted to interfere so far as even to say, " I tolerate you? I tolerate your Independency,—your Episcopacy,—your Presbyterianism: you are a Baptist, but I tolerate you." There is an insult implied, it has been said, in the way in which the liberty purports to be granted. It bestows as a boon what already exists as a right. We want no despot to tell us that he gives us leave to breathe the free air of heaven, or that he permits us to worship God agreeably to the dictates of our conscience. Such are the views with which a majority of the British people regard, in these latter times, the right to tolerate; and regarding a *right* NOT to tolerate, they must be more decided still. The Free Church, then, must lay her complaint before them. She must tell them, that such is the oppression to which her people are subjected, that she would be but too happy to see even the beggarly elements of the question recognised in their behalf,—that she would be but too happy to hear the despot of a province pronounce the deprecated " I tolerate you," seeing that his virtual enunciation at present is, " I do NOT tolerate you," and seeing that he is powerful enough, through a misapplication of his rights and influence, as the most extensive of British proprietors, to give terrible effect to the unjust and illiberal determination. The Free Church, on this question, must raise her appeal everywhere to public opinion, and we entertain no doubt that she will everywhere find it her friend.

But how is its power to be directed? How bring it to bear upon the Duke of Sutherland? It is an all-potent lever, but it must be furnished with a fulcrum on which to rest, and a direction in which to bear. Let us remark, first, that no signal privilege or right was ever yet achieved for Britain, that was not preceded by some signal wrong. From the times of Magna Charta down to the times of the Revolution, we find every triumph of liberty heralded in by some gross outrage upon it. The history of the British Constitution is a history of great natural rights established piecemeal under the immediate promptings of an indignation elicited by unbearable wrongs. It was not until the barrier that protected the privileges of the citizen from the will of the despot, gave way at some weak point, that the parties exposed to the inundation were roused up to re-erect it on a better principle and a surer foundation. Now, the Duke of Sutherland (with some of his brother proprietors) has just succeeded in showing us a signal flaw in our scheme of religious toleration, and this at an exceedingly critical time. He has been perpetrating a great and palpable wrong, which, if rightly represented, must have the effect of leading men, in exactly the old mode, to arouse themselves in behalf of the corresponding right. If a single proprietor can virtually do what the Sovereign of Great Britain would forfeit the crown for barely attempting to do,—if a single nobleman can do what the House of Lords in its aggregate capacity would peril its very existence for but proposing to do,—then does there exist in the British Constitution a palpable flaw, which cannot be too soon remedied. There must be a weak place in the barrier, if the waters be rushing out; and it cannot be too soon rebuilt on a surer plan. Here, then, evidently, is the point on which the generated opinion ought to be brought to bear. It has as its proper arena the political field. It is a defect in the British Constitution, strongly exemplified by the case of Sutherland, that the rights of property may be so stretched as to overbear the rights of conscience,—that though toleration be the law of the country generally, it may be so set aside by the country's proprietary, as not to be the law in any particular part of it; and to reverse this state of things,—to make provision in the Constitution, that the rights of the proprietor be not so overstretched, and that a virtual repeal of the toleration laws in any part of the country be not possible,—are palpably the objects to which the public mind should be directed.

We have said, that the Duke of Sutherland has succeeded in showing us this flaw in the Constitution at a peculiarly critical time. A gentleman resident in England, for whose judgment we entertain the highest respect, told us only a few days since, that the rising, all-absorbing party of that kingdom, so far at least as the Established Church and the aristocracy are concerned, still continues to be the Puseyite party. If Puseyism does not bid fair to possess a majority of the people of the country, it bids fair at least to possess a majority of its acres. And we need scarce remind the reader how peculiarly this may be the case with Scotland, whose acres, in such large proportions, are under the control of an incipient Puseyism already. In both countries, therefore, is it of peculiar importance, in a time like the present, that the law of toleration should be placed beyond the control of a hostile or illiberal proprietary,—so placed beyond their control, that they may be as unable virtually to suspend its operation in any part of the country, as they already are to suspend its operation in the whole of the country. We are recommending, be it remembered, no wild scheme of Chartist aggression on the rights of property,—we would but injure our cause by doing so: our strength in this question must altogether depend on the soundness of the appeal which we can carry to the natural justice of the community. We merely recommend that that be done in behalf of the already recognised law of toleration, which Parliament has no hesitation in doing in behalf of some railway or canal, or water or dock company, when, for what is deemed a public good, it sets aside the absolute control of the proprietor over at least a portion of his property, and consigns it at a fair price to the corporation engaged in the undertaking. The principle of the scheme is already recognised by the Constitution, and its legislative embodiment would be at once easy and safe. Property would be rendered not less, but more secure, if, in every instance in which a regularly-organized congregation of any denomination of Christians to which the law of toleration itself extended, made application for ground on which to erect a place of worship, the application would be backed and made effectual, in virtue of an enacted law, by the authority of the Constitution. There is no Scotch or English Dissenter,—no true friend of religious liberty, in Britain or Ireland,—who would not make common cause with the Free Church in urging a measure of this character on Parliament, when fairly convinced, by cases such as that of Sutherland, how imperatively such a measure is required.

Unavoidably, however, from the nature of things, the relief which ultimately may be thus secured cannot be other than distant relief. Much information must first be spread, and the press and the platform extensively employed. Can there be nothing done for Sutherland through an already existing political agency? We are of opinion there can. Sutherland itself is even more thoroughly a *close* county now, than it was ere the Reform Bill had swamped the paper votes, and swept away the close burghs. His Grace the Duke has but to nominate his member, and his member is straightway returned. But all the political power which, directly or indirectly, his Grace possesses, is not equally secure. Sutherland is a close county; but the Northern Burghs are not rotten burghs; on the contrary, they possess an independent and intelligent constituency; and in scarce any part of Scotland is the Free Church equally strong. And his Grace derives no inconsiderable portion of his political influence from them. The Member for Sutherland is virtually his Grace's nominee, but the Member for the Northern Burghs is not his Grace's nominee at all; and yet certain it is that the gentleman by whom these burghs are at present represented in Parliament is his Grace's agent and adviser in all that pertains to the management of Sutherland, and has been so for many years. His Grace's Member for Sutherland sits in Parliament in virtue of being his Grace's nominee; but the sort of Prime Minister through which his Grace governs his princely domains, sits in Parliament, not in virtue of being his Grace's nominee, but in virtue of his being himself a man of liberal opinions, and an enemy to all intolerance. He represents them in the Whig interest, and in his character as a Whig. His Grace would very soon have one member less in Parliament, did that member make common cause with his Grace in suppressing the Free Church in Sutherland. Now, the bruit shrewdly goeth, that that member does make common cause with his Grace. The bruit shrewdly goeth, that in this, as in most other matters, his Grace acts upon that member's advice. True, the report may be altogether idle,—it may be utterly without foundation; instead of being true, it may be exactly the reverse of being true; but most unquestionable it is, that, whether true or otherwise, it exists, and that that member's constituency have a very direct interest in it. He represents them miserably ill, and must be a very different sort of Whig from them, if he hold that proprietors do right in virtually setting aside the Toleration Act. The report does one of two things,—it either does him great injustice, or it shows that he has sat too long in Parliament for the Northern Burghs. It is in the power, then, of the highly respectable and intelligent Whig constituency of this district to make such a diversion in favour of the oppressed people of Sutherland, as can scarce fail to tell upon the country, and this in thorough consistency with the best and highest principles of their party. Let them put themselves in instant communication with their member, and, stating the character of the report which so generally exists to his prejudice, request a categorical answer regarding it ;—let them request an avowal of his opinion of the Duke's policy, equally articulate with that opinion which the Hon. Mr Fox Maule submitted to the public a few weeks ago in the columns of the *Witness;*— and then, as the ascertained circumstances of the case may direct, let them act, and that publicly, in strict accordance with their principles. Of one thing they may be assured,—the example will tell.

In order to raise the necessary amount of opinion for carrying the ulterior object,—the enactment of a law,—there are various most justifiable expedients to which the friends of toleration in the country should find it not difficult to resort. Petitions addressed to the Lower House in its legislative capacity, and to the members of the Upper House as a body of men who have, perhaps, of all others, the most direct stake in the matter,—we need scarce say how,—ought, of course, to take a very obvious place on the list. Much too might be done by deputations from the General Assembly of the Free Church, instructed from time to time to ascertain, and then publicly to report on, the state of Sutherland. Each meeting of the Assembly might be addressed on the subject by some of its ablest men, in which case their statements and speeches would go forth, through the medium of the press, to the country at large. The co-operation and assistance of all bodies of Evangelical Dissenters, both at home and abroad, should be sedulously sought after, and correct information on the subject circulated among them extensively. There has been much sympathy elicited for the Church, during her long struggle, among good men everywhere. Her cause has been tried, and judgment given in her favour, in France, Holland, and America, and in not a few of the colonies. In the case of Sismondi, " On the *Clearing* of Sutherland," we see the opinion of a Continental philosopher re-echoed back upon our own country, not without its marked effect ; and it might be well to try whether the effect of foreign opinion might not be at least equally influential " On the Suppression of the Toleration Laws in Sutherland." There is one great country with which we hold our literature in common, and which we can address, and by which we can be in turn addressed, in our native tongue. Unluckily, what ought to have existed as a bond of union and amity has been made to subserve a very different purpose ; and we cannot conceal from ourselves the fact, that our own country has been mainly to blame. The manners, habits, and tastes of the Americans have been exhibited by not a few of our popular writers, in the broadest style of caricature ; they have been described as a nation of unprincipled speculators, devoid not only of right feeling, but even of common honesty, and remarkable for but their scoundrelism and conceit. Even were such descriptions just, which they are not, most assuredly would they be unwise. It is the American people, rather than the American Government, who make peace and war ; and the first American war with England will be one of the most formidable in which this country has yet been engaged. The bowie-knife is no trifling weapon ; and the English writer laughs at a very considerable expense, if his satires have the effect of whetting it. At present, however, the war between the two countries is but a war of libel and pasquinade, and the advantage hitherto has been on the side of the aggressor. America has not been happy in her retaliation. We would fain direct her to aim, where her darts, instead of provoking national hostility, or exciting a bitter spirit among the entire people of a country, would but subserve the general cause of liberty and human improvement. It is but idle to satirize our manners and customs ; we think them good. There is nothing to be gained by casting ridicule on our peculiar modes of thinking ; they are the modes to which we have been accustomed, and we prefer them to any others. But there are matters of a different kind, regarding which the country bears a conscience, and is not quite at its ease ; and there we are vulnerable. We speak often, we would fain say, of slavery in your country, literati of America, and justly deem it a great evil. It might do us good were you to remind us, in turn, that there are extensive districts in our own, in which virtually there exists no toleration law for the religion of the people, though that religion be Protestantism in its purest form. Cast your eyes upon the county of Sutherland.

RESOLUTION FOR PUBLIC MEETINGS.—" That humble petitions be presented to both Houses of Parliament, and to the Queen's Majesty, praying that they would be graciously pleased to pass into a law any measure which may be brought into either of the Houses of the Legislature, having for its object the extension into that part of the united kingdom called Sutherland, of the privileges of religious toleration to the extent they are enjoyed by her Majesty's subjects in other parts of the empire."

APPENDIX.

THE following letters, interesting in themselves, and doubly so from what they illustrate, must be regarded as valuable corroborations of the character of the 93d or Sutherland Highlanders, given in our second chapter. The first,—that from a field-officer,—seems to have been suggested by the chapter itself, which, like all the others, appeared as an article in the *Witness* newspaper ; but the second,—that from a non-commissioned officer of the 93d,—could not possibly have been prompted by it, as it dates from Kingston, in Canada, only six days after the article had been published in Edinburgh.

"MR EDITOR,—Reminiscences of the times gone by will occasionally intrude upon an old soldier, and my attention has been more particularly caught by an admirable article in your "*Witness*" of Wednesday last, upon the state of the Highlands of Sutherland some years ago ; and the pain it has given to you, and to every well-wisher of the remote part of our county, to find that the Duke has refused to grant sites or stances for the Free Presbyterian Church. That such things should be (I was going to say tolerated) in this the 19th century, is all but incredible, and I envy not the feeling that prompts it.

"The Highlands of Sutherland, though a barren and 'heath clad' district, yet have ever been found fertile in producing hardy and gallant men, able and willing to do their country good service. In proof of this, I would particularly allude to the 93d or Sutherland Highland regiment. It was my fate to witness that excellent corps go into action at the taking of the Cape of Good Hope, 8th January 1806; and although the brilliancy of the day was clouded by the upsetting of a boat containing the grenadier company of the 93d, and the consequent loss of nearly forty fine fellows, who had just taken off their bonnets to cheer at being the first regiment to land in face of the enemy,—yet the steadiness of their formation and advance, under a heavy fire, was admirable. But it is not so much to this, which, methinks, is common to all regiments, but more particularly to the very exemplary conduct of the men in garrison during the five years I was Brigade Major there, and which called forth the repeated commendation of Sir David Baird and of General Grey,—two strict disciplinarians. There was something in the 93d which somehow could not be attained in the steady old English regiment to which I belonged, nor in any other regiment I have ever known. It was, in fact, a sort of family corps ; for when any inattention to orders or breach of discipline occurred, the captain had only to say, that he 'would send home a report of Donald's misbehaviour to the minister of the parish,' and this had an effect upon the Sutherland Highlander beyond any sentence of a court-martial. The sums of money remitted regularly to their parents in the Highlands was also remarkable, and bespoke the good feeling imbibed in early youth. In a service of thirty-two years in all quarters of the world, and having met with almost every regiment in the service, from the grenadier guards down to West India and Hottentot corps, I never met with such men as composed the Sutherland Highland regiment. It was at that time a regiment perfectly unique, and probably is so now. And shall it be said, Mr Editor, that the fathers and the children of such men shall be denied the privilege of worshipping the God of their fathers upon their own soil, in any way that their conscience bids them! Forbid it, heaven! And should such a system be persevered in by any landlord, let his name be held up to Europe,—to humanity all over the world,—to that detestation and abhorrence which such an uncalled-for prohibition, such an assumption of authority, justly merits.

"The hard-fought action in front of New Orleans, and the painful list of killed and wounded in the 93d, attest the persevering bravery of the Sutherland High-

9 781276 040662